BEYOND THE ORDINARY

TALES OF THE IMAGINATION

PRASHANTH GHATTADAHALLY

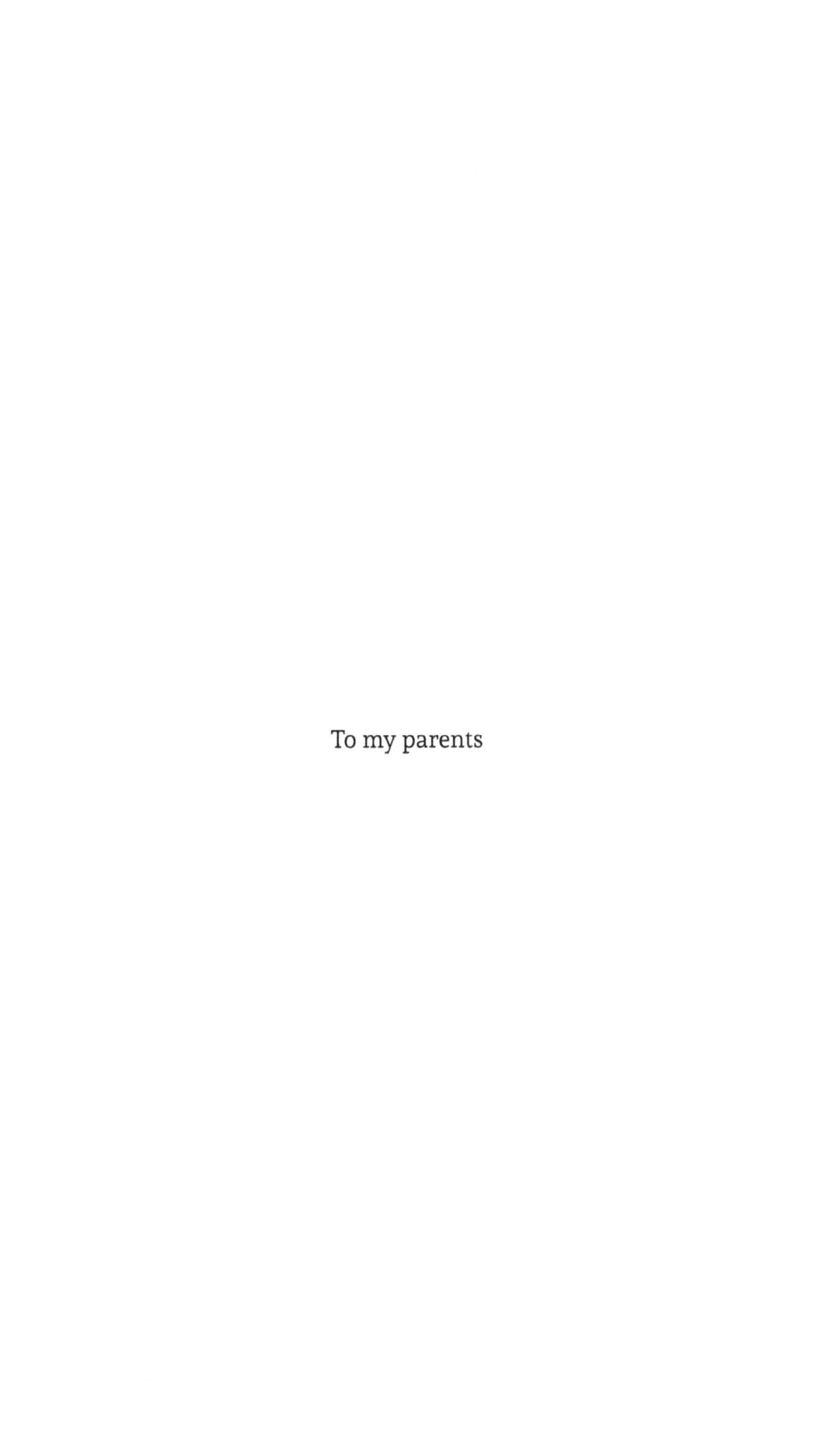

To my parents

Contents

Preface

Only the human of all the creations of the God is benefitted with a super and yet complex organ called Mind. We seldom use the mind for run of the mill matters like family matters, weddings, planning a vacation, beating the pressure etc. A common man always avoids different ways to explore the hidden treasures of mind. Thinking is cheap and doesnt need one to go to Himalayas or some remotest forest to imgaine things. A common can sail through the crazy lingering thoughts while walking in a park, or enjoying is drive etc. This book is one such collection of thoughts of a common man captured as is.

This book began as a simple idea, a seed planted during a late-night conversation with friends about the stories we carry with us—the ones we tell, the ones we live, and the ones we keep buried deep within. It was during that conversation that I realized how often we overlook the quiet, hidden narratives that shape our lives. The story that follows is a collection of those moments, woven together into a larger tapestry. It is not a grand tale of heroes and villains, but rather a reflection on the choices we make, the paths we take, and the people we become along the way. It explores the spaces between certainty and doubt, where our true selves are often revealed.

As you read, you may recognize parts of your own journey within these pages. You may find yourself nodding in agreement, or perhaps questioning the decisions of the characters. My hope is that this book resonates with you in some way, that it sparks a memory, a feeling, or a thought that lingers long after the last page is turned.

Thank you for joining me on this journey. Whether you laugh, complain, or simply reflect, I hope this story touches you in a way that feels honest and true.

ᗐᗐᗐ

With Gratitude,
    Prashanth Ghattadahally

Acknowledgements

Writing a book is not a solo journey and often involves conversations with many thankless friends and family and especially my wife Nandini, who tolerated my half-cooked diaglogues about all the crazy stuff. My daughter Pavani, for still instilling me a curiosity to cherish little things about life.

Prologue

All characters in this book are entirely fictional. Any resemblance to actual persons, living or dead, is purely coincidental.

1
A Week as a Day

Have you ever heard about the time differences between Earth's time units and those in other star systems? It's said that on some planets, a single day is equivalent to an entire year here on Earth. This phenomenon occurs due to complex factors like time dimensions and the relative distances to the Sun and other stars. But wait—why would we need to travel so far to observe such time lags? Aren't we already seeing our weeks turning into days? How is that even possible on Earth?

Let me introduce you to an English word called "evening"! Sounds strange, aah don't call me crazy or a belabor saying obvious things. Times keep changing and a few words would lose their original significance gradually and deserve a different narration. They get reduced merely to the Oxford dictionaries from real experiences. Henceforth, "evening" is such a word which invites for consideration from the new generation of us.

How many of us remember those authentic sun sets with the soothing golden rays, or those playful evenings of childhood or casual visits to friends and relatives for a cup of coffee and lazing around with snacks in the evenings?

The evening was the most relaxing part of our extensive day. Let me factor my experiences with those wonderful evenings, and I'm pretty sure most of you would recount some experiences with mine.

Formerly, we lived in a solitary house referred to as "Thotada mane" by the folks (a garden house in Kannada, visibly medium house built by the ancestors who preferred life with nature over hustles of civilization). The house was situated right next to the fields overlooking a garden covering thickets of coco nut and beetle trees. Being a joint family, there were easily more than 15 members including servants living under the same roof. Our elders mostly sourced their incomes from teaching and agricultural professions.

So, how were the evenings then?

Oh don't ask, they were just heavenly. Most delightful experience was standing on the long running platform before the house, peeking out with anxious eyes for the sight of returning cattle from the graze, hearing to the sounds of bells tied to their necks, bunch of countrymen trailing these animals with their ploughs and other agricultural instruments. The dusky environment painted the scene nearly perfect! The heads of the family would couch around the platform reciprocating their experiences of the day, sipping on the hot Kaapi (coffee in Kannada) and spending the next 2-3 hours in all the chit chat. Further to the company was the pleasant sight of the coco nuts trees rattling to the evening winds, croaking frogs and the buzzing insects.

Fortunately, there were no Television and not even electricity in the house in the earlier days. Largely, the evening was spent in socializing and nothing more. More than the longish day, the shorter evenings were more rewarding, wanting, soothing and igniting the feeling of warmth and belonging in the family.

On special occasions, what's stationed in the memory is the folks braving up to the honeycomb rooted trees in the late evenings carrying a torch, a bucket, a matchbox and adequate clothes to cover their faces. They were mostly successful with their untaught experience of removing honey from the combs. This involved local methods like generating the smoke plentiful to shun away the bees for leaving behind their nectar.

Days passed by, as we got our first electricity experience at the house! The government had to drag the wires from almost 5 kms only to light up our little house. Not the best in the beginning, the power was limited only to the evenings. There was a pump house, and evening was the only opportunity to water the nearby crops like sugarcane and maize. The funny part was the kids joining in the company of the seniors only to create chaos, make noises and do nothing useful. Water was all over the place when the kids made the mess by not able to control their excitement over channeling the water, rushing away from the pipes.

As the evening rolls out and the slight darkness kicks in, kids had to start circling around the kerosene lamps for their studies with no surety of the fluctuating power. What an experience to chuck away from the books, those little-known insects struggling to make their way into the tiny lamps.

Dinner was a feast every day, with more than 10 people sitting around in the order of seniority on the floor. What a delight it was, watching the seniors gulping the ragi balls with one down push, which was the hardest part of the meal course for the kids. Oops, sorry got carried away to dinner time from evening, let me come back. As though it was not enough, servants in the house would set bonfires near the house during winters. Who would not care for the adventurous stories firing up the adventurism in us wanting to grow up fast?

ᐳᐳᐳ

The next adventurous part started after joining a primary school which needs you to tread nearly 2 kms from the house. Out of many moments, what stuck the most was the gang of kids wading their ways through the curvy bunds of the paddy fields and then crossing over tiny streams before reaching home. Noises made were enough to shove away any hiding wild animals behind the bushes (not so wild during our age, may be a few jackals and dogs). The walk was incomplete without the scary thoughts in mind walking by the side of a burial ground, especially during evenings once you leave the town. The company of kids was great with elder cousin brothers, lovely sister and other neighboring kids. Some unpleasant yet funny moments when someone unexpectedly fenced entry into their private lands on the way back, leaving us to wander and find newer ways to reach our own home!

Moving on, my next date in the evening started after moving into a small heritage town by the side of river Yagachi for the middle schooling. A little degrade from earlier beautiful evenings, however every situation in life won't leave you empty handed if you ask for it. Opened our eyes slowly to the town culture, to the vehicles, restless kids and packed houses. The best experience of the town was playing hide-and-seek behind numerous idols of the magnificent ancient temple on every Thursday's evening visit. The one-rupee per hour-rented bicycle visits to the outskirts of the town for the river bridge, walking up to the dam construction sites were very memorable evenings.

Shifted to the district headquarters for higher schooling and colleges. Being part of a bigger town, population was quite sizable, however surprisingly there was no nuisance of mad traffic with those honky vehicles. Every part of the town was reachable well within 10 mins on a moped! The famous Mutt Road of the town used to get eventful with most faces from the college thronging it by the evening. Couldn't get away without hanging around with friends, or a quick munching of the famous chats and a gaze of our personal interests walking around! One would not return without walking down the street umpteen times only to be left with so much time in the evening! Then, all you needed was just 10 damn mins to be back home after having fun.

At present living in the metro, an evening is something which is entirely underestimated for its worth. The only authentic evening one gets to familiarize with is over a Friday! Can we say the week starts over a Monday, don't stop anywhere in anticipation for a Friday evening. All you get rewarded is just one single evening in a week!

In this logic, can we say, a week runs like one busy long day with a single morning and a single evening. The middle part of the week/day is spent working and preparing for the fears of the unknown future? So, have we lost the idea of a week which has time-lagged and reduced to one virtual day!!

Thanks to the Vitamin D tests, one can find the sunlight deprived funny faces (including me) struggling to get a glimpse of the single most rays of sun in the morning or evenings.

Can we retrieve the evenings one more time before the final sun set of our life?

2
The Selection

A batch is ready to be dispatched to Mother Earth to be born again, to lead their well earnt lives; to be born in the wombs of kind women nurturing splendid dreams of conceiving a wonderful child with their husbands. This is a blissful day for the batch as they finally succeeded in winning this birth after a long struggle and hard negotiation with lawmakers at some remote transitory planet. The batch is called the "batch" due to the similarities they shared in terms of upcoming deeds, a complete package or manuscript of what lies ahead of them, on how the fortune wheels would turn for them and many more secrets!

Look at the premise of the "Great Ground" which is a large place in the magnificent city of "Amura" on the remotest planet of Theta Galaxy, a billion Light years away from Mother Earth. The law makers have announced the final round of negotiation among the chosen lot. There is no selection, only the brave volunteers seeking birth on Earth are chosen for the Negotiation. The volunteers have been asked to fill their forms with such pristine details captivated by their choices in country, religion, faith, caste, race, wealth, health/disease, family, spouse, children and grandchildren (if possible) and last but not the least their appearance! It looks very simple right! SOL1027 was one such volunteer, who grabbed the piece of paper called Form 21 from Mr. Ante Noyce (the chief lawmaker) with great confidence. SOL1027 wrote complete details without wasting any time; for he was so prepared for this occasion. Alas, Rejection!

Was Mr. Ante Noyce truly so heartless that he couldn't approve a simple birth request form for SOL1027, especially when the volunteer had waited for years? These days, negotiations are becoming increasingly rare, thanks to Earth's agents' tight control over space. The Earth's agents of birth are frustrated with the overwhelming population—there's nothing left to feed the masses, no places to sleep, and no land left to cultivate. Earth has devolved into a chaotic mess, ravaged by wars, corruption, and global warming. It's no longer a paradise. As a result, the office of Earth's agents has grown more conservative, particularly when it comes to approving negotiations. Either the elderly are living longer, thanks to groundbreaking medicines, or the new life forms—eggs frozen in cold storage for years—remain untouched, with no caretakers in sight.

Contrary to the initial belief that Mr. Ante Noyce had personally rejected the request, SOL1027 is stunned to discover the rejection seal stamped by the batch of volunteers, with 75% voting against it. What's going on here? How could lawmakers allow batchmates to vote when they might want you to fail? "Mr. Ante Noyce, could you kindly explain?" asks SOL1027, hoping for some clarity.

"No, sorry, I can't explain," Noyce replies coldly. "Ask your batch. The reality is, you weren't selected because you didn't include a buffer for no match on Earth. The truth is, there's no place on Earth that aligns with your form."

SOL1027, aghast, responds, "Oh, my heavens, what am I supposed to do now? Should I just wait for ages for the next round of negotiations?"

"Nope, don't get depressed, you have failed like most of your batchmates. As a matter of fact, nobody clears Form 21, it's rather a fake form. It doesn't work like that. The real negotiation begins now". "Ok are you going to lend me a new form then? Wow". "Nope, there is no new form. The round has no registry of forms, neither there is voting nor there is a selection or rejection. There's no round of competition with the batch as there is no one watching you and reviewing your form. "Mr. Ante Noyce, please don't confuse me, this is not a joke, you can't imagine how have I waited and deserved this negotiation day. I wouldn't mind the voting by the batch and ready to abide by their verdict. Let's play the game straight. Ok?"

"See it starts with Form 21 only to make you aware that Selection is not a cheap and careless procedure. You get what you reap. Let me not lecture you on Karma – a baggage of your good / bad deeds amassed over previous encounters on Earth! We are not lawmakers but only agents facilitating your negotiation with your own self. We are not negotiators and have no database of your actions or karma calculations. We don't know you at all!

As a matter of fact, this round of negotiation is only chosen by you at the end of the last occasion. The law maker or the agent is ostensibly chosen by you. Don't forget, only you have the database of your own deeds saved in your locker. You bring them here and open the suitcase of hibernated memories. We will provide you with a magnificent theatre with a large LED screen with you as the audience. You are asked to watch your movie and judge your actions. You can bring your friends as you wish but we don't generally recommend that".

"OK, what happens when a movie is played. How about pausing to go back and play again?".

"Good question. You have the controls but remember there is no fast forward. If you go back, it just plays again and again. Now, coming to the most important question, what happens after you watch the movie right? This is where you decide on your merits and drawbacks. You may want to have a birth in the house of Walmart or Ambani. Or marry the most beautiful woman on Earth and lead rest of the life doing nothing on a paradise island right? But does your consciousness approve of that?".

"Hmm, Now I get your words. But let me tell you, I am not a devoted person, but I am a big manipulative. What if I compromise my consciousness and select the best of birth?"

"No, you will be asked to score on your movie at every critical scene / event of your life. The movie is interactive and doesn't move to the next scene without having your score recorded along".

"Oh, come on, now you have revealed all the secrets! Why should I score less than average. I would rank myself the maximum and fool you right. So, what's the real fun here?

"Ok my friend, if you are done with all your questions, let me share with you a rule of the funny game. The memory of our conversation is also erased before you watch the movie. Remember this is only a transitory planet and doesn't register your actions or memories. You will never realize that you are watching your own movie. Instead, you are made to believe that you are watching and scoring your batch mate's movie. Believe me, you would never compromise consciousness and instead come up with fair scores in complete neutrality.

In a nutshell you have now successfully reviewed your own movie unknowingly – i.e. your own deeds of past life and produced the score card.

The score card is very elusive as it finds a reasonable home for next birth. It matches the most complex of equations to select the best match in terms of cast, family, country, place etc. for your next birth on Earth. Remember, the whole negotiation round is complete only when the agents of Earth create space for you and if the Green and peaceful Mother Earth waits for you!

Ok, now since you have lost the memory of this conversation too, shall we go to the movie theater for the scoring, my friend".

"Kumar, why don't you accelerate, we are getting late for the wedding reception".

Mr. Kumar woke up from deep thoughts and continued accelerating for the rest of the journey to reach the destination.

Mr. Kumar had started off with the family attending a wedding in a nearby town in the evening. Normally it shouldn't take a couple of hours to reach the place unless you are negotiating with the enduring construction work for the metro and other traffic chaos.

The car plays an important role in Kumar's life and it's not exaggerating to be entitled as his second home! Thanks to the busy routine of our generation, who has time to conduct a decent conversation longing more than 10 minutes. Glued to personal gadgets or books etc. are not uncommon scenes in our homes. However, Car does the trick for you. Not only does it put everyone compulsorily together for few hours in a lesser place but also brings that connect and urge for talking.

After initial hours of chit chat, music and laughter, the destination still looked far away thanks to the average pace of Kumar's small car, which is also being overtaken by overspeeding SUVs on the road. With the kids gradually taken over by the cool games on the phone and wife gliding into sleep, it left Kumar to perform only one function i.e. drive peacefully.

Having left to his own self amusement, unusual thoughts started filling Kumar's mind today. Thoughts drifted away from the destination, the wedding to the tunes of universe, the motion, the balance and all centered on the car itself. There are plenty of rules and regulations to follow while driving, like having no alcohol, following the lanes, watching for speed breakers etc. Conversely there is no restriction yet on putting brakes in thinking or imagining. Count on me, it's not a surprise when being alarmed by the software on the car in future for over thinking or imagining by reading the face gestures.

How does a car start? What is a torque and why do we need the horse power? One good thing that most car drivers enjoy is accelerating on an unobstructed empty road. Nothing is ideal, of course brakes are needed. So, which is important here? The ignition, the acceleration or the brakes? All are vital for a perfect drive!

Oh Gosh! What's that one common product of the above combination? It's the balance. Once the car is set in motion, nobody counts the times powering the acceleration or the brakes? No, it's next to impossible. It's uncommon for someone to drive with the conscious mind always, as something from us keeps the momentum giving, doing a perfect maneuver of the acceleration and braking all the time. Probably one would have noticed braking or accelerating only during initial days of learning but not when you have understood the game.

What's astounding is the fact there are 100' of cars being driven on the same road at a given point meaning there are 100s of balanced products in motion. So, what's our relation to them? We don't know any of them, yet we trust their balances but shout (honk) when someone loses balance and interferes in our privacy ahead.

ppp

Let's make an analogy behind this theory of motion and where it all got started?

Notwithstanding being such a wonderful machine, a car is of no use when put at rest. It's no different from any other piece of metal. No matter how many journeys you make, and clocked 1000's of kilometers, a car is as good as the next journey it makes. Henceforward it's not wrong to say, a car is born every time you begin a new journey. It has fuel and a magnificent body to begin with. Truly the car is born upon its ignition from the key. The ignition unites the extremely potential fuel with the static engine giving birth to a force ready to rock n roll.

If you consider the body or the engine of the car as "Shiva" and the amazing hidden energy, the fuel as the "Shakti", the ignition just paved way for the great union of them creating the dance of Shiva and Shakti, in other words "Shivashakti". Who started the car? The spark which is the initiator or the creator of this journey. What fun in having an expensive car which doesn't start. The ignition as the creator of the journey plays a crucial role as "Brahma".

Is that all needed to move. No, here comes the important part. You have all the gear with you and that needs to be invoked for the motion. But a 3rd or a 4th, 5th gear cannot begin the journey though being powerful. One needs to go through the initial "first" step which is the 1st or 2nd gear.

This demands the first action i.e. famously called as "Ganesha" receiving the first offering in any journey.

All set to go, now the fun starts for a passionate driver. The car starts and put into transit with the initial gears, the whole road is lying ahead, what's stopping us. Boom! Press the accelerator and start speeding. Never realized when we slide into 3rd, 4th so on. The state of motion is maintained by gears and acceleration. Let's call the acceleration as "Vishnu" who keeps the "stithi" with the road and keeps the state of motion.

Next is predictable right! Life is not ideal, remember we talked about producing balance from the car. There are other drivers on the road, one cannot keep accelerating all the while. Breaks are needed to check the momentum and keep resetting. Why don't we call braking as "laya" and offer it to "Maheswara".

If everything is going well, what's the issue? Heard of deadly accidents? What causes this? Good guess, the change in balance, over ambition for speed or fate loses the balance of "srushti", "stiti", "laya" and invites the ultimatum. "Kali" or "Rudra" play their part role and end the journey. Wishing everyone a good safe balance, let's move on to the next point.

Normally, the journeys can stop with graceful action of "laya" by themselves with the braking in normal form and the ignition turned off. This puts the car back into the original state of rest. The "srusti", "stiti" and "laya", "Prathama" or the "creator" all disappear and make no relevance now. What remains is a state of nothingness and union with the original state. i.e. "Parabrahma".

Did we start with "Parabrahma" before, let's do it now. The journey of the car was possible only when the right enablers acted at right time. However, all played their part only when summoned by someone else. Then who is the master giving commands unmistakably all the time. It's you! You are the force behind actioning these elements. Only the key roles are considered here for the analogy skipping all other enablers with due respect, such as the fire from combustion, the earth in the form of the road ahead, the wind for combustion again and external influence, the water in the fuel and the sky for creating the space of expanding the journey.

Neither the car nor the drivers have relevance unless the journey is born. The pieces of Parabrahma take part in the creation of new journeys or universes from somewhere in space. Only a few have understood from where they are cast and where they are put back in the state of nothingness.

"Yes baba", we are set to reach before the reception starts." Replies Mr. Kumar.

4

The Queue

There is a relation between points and a straight line. While the line connects two ends, points fill up the line. A line cannot exist without points! While it's hard to imagine which side the line is headed, it's the direction of points that matters here. But what's intriguing is, who decides the direction of the points? Do the points resolve themselves or is there someone commanding? Or is it community behavior? Also have you seen a line with only a single point in it. Then why do we care for the line only the point which is relevant here. There is a paradox.

One can imagine a queue as a straight line composed of people standing as points, there is no queue without the aspirants lined up. When was the last time we remember standing in a queue? A queue is a significant connection from one state of our physical existence to the other. A queue gets over only to put us in the next one. Many find the queue was unnecessary after a while. For instance, you don't need a queue to look at the sun or moon! Let's explore some acquaintances of queues in our life!

Going back in chronological order, who would forget queuing up to ATMs during demonetization days. Standing in the queue for a mere 2000 rupees and again for another 2000! Sometimes they have carried multiple cards only to get yelled at by the people behind who would make the same mistake! Leaving behind the verdict of what's right or wrong to the TV panelists, this is one famous queue stood by the whole nation from a businessman to a daily wager. The queue almost got on our nerves when the ATMs got dry just before your turn! The queue was unarguably the longest and the largest ever stood by mankind considering the size of our country!

Next, the queue for our kids' admission to school, rather I would prefer to refer to this as the queue of emotions. The popular schools in the area amazingly tested their patience before declaring the kids' entry results! While many schools still offered a no-queue decent admission, the ego made us queue for the celebrity ones. The best part was the ability of the parents to get into a full circle of anxiety, fear, and rush only to pay hefty sums of money into the pockets of school management. Not going to the details of queues at passport office, immigration & security checks at airports which are quite customary these days, anyways a recent spread of virus has started clearing up this mess too. The funny part of the queue at the airports is the rush to get frisked by the cops only to confirm you are a normal flyer!

Other funny moments of standing in a queue of our times was to get vaccinated at primary schools (not in recent times), where the kids performed every possible method to get away from the target. So a queue does not always stand craving the target, sometimes you are put in a queue for the good which is immediately not known to you! On the contrary, we would be standing in a queue voluntarily aspiring to get at something which is not truly worth the wait. For instance, a senior citizen standing in a queue at a bank only to get an entry at pass books! An overly ambitious guy going for a third serving at a buffet, a queue for the first day first show of a super star movie causing stampedes sometimes, and many more to quote.

What is a queue? When a person does the same things his/her peers are doing, a queue becomes inevitable. A queue is only a way to throttle the rush from people attaining a new state in their life. Whether it's financial stability or social status, the queue becomes unavoidable to move forward in life. Wait, do we really need to move forward? Is the queue always one directional? All the references mentioned above explain queuing existences from the physical world. But how about self-imposed queues in our virtual existence? Have we gotten so accustomed to ending up queuing, without noticing that a queue is not necessary all the time?

How many times do we dream of emulating a great personality, or certain aspects that we want to achieve in this lifetime? Life goes on, but the target keeps moving too. Not undermining the fact that we chase our dreams and move closer, however, it's no less than an eternal queue. Specifically, it's not a secret that we have started spending more time with ourselves to understand the real person behind. Pondering over what lies in the vastness of the ocean of our mind, for only to make wise decisions. But is that so simple? Why are we surrounded by so many Gurus if it were so simple? There is no dearth of videos or books penned by great personality coaches these days, but no one can claim to stand in our private queue of seeking wisdom. It's no less than a private queue to us than any other external target mentioned above!

But why do we stand in this private selfie queue? The basic fact that takes us forward is the notion that life is one directional. For a moment, let's consider we are unlearning everything that we possessed in the beginning by exhausting reserves. For instance, many say the kids have extreme ability to grasp things, being able to see what they see, hear what they hear and do what they want to. Noises in the sounds, thoughts and sight have fooled us to think that we are moving forward. Why don't we reverse the source and targets and put the queue upside down?

Going even further, when you turn back to chat with by standers in the selfie queue, you would be stunned to find no one behind or frontward! As there is only one person footing the queue. Ironically, the target of the queue is not different from the very person standing. What an irony, a person standing in the queue for his whole life (or next) only to meet himself. Wise people have relatively advanced their private queues, and many are yet to start. Essentially, the queue is not obligatory as there lies a single point through line. The "point" which is "us", is already born united with the target also. Why don't we remove the queue, start being what we are already today than endeavoring to stand up the non-existent queue! As some someone said, the best day of life is today. It's happening already! A queue might be a myth making us nothing less than a flock of sheep summoned to move forward.

5

Watching you

After going through the painful experiences of two consecutive years of Covid, many families were returning to normalcy. Thanking the Almighty for whoever left in the family, for keeping one alive to narrate the stories to the future generations and feeling proud of being dearer and nearer to the Gods they loved and prayed.

But who knows the ways of God, one who dismisses every belief in a flash of 2 seconds, every fortune that you thought earned by several years of prayers, by visiting temples or performing the virtuous deeds.

I will tell you a story of a village being struck by floods for consecutive years. The villagers did everything to save themselves from the ferocious river. They built checks and dams, prepared lifesaving boats and sent the old and sick to the far away safe havens. This worked for years, but not until doomsday when the swelling river swept away everything on the village leaving nothing to the remains. With great difficulty the villagers managed to sail the river with the help of lifeboats and reached the safe shores. After surviving the loss of several people in the sail, the leftover villagers landed on the shore and thanked the Gods in every possible way!

Surviving such an ordeal, they thought there was nothing that came in between them and the prosperous fortunes waiting for them. Mr. Aralis were one such family, having witnessed many misfortunes already in their life, strongly believed they will be luckiest to be spared by the Gods in every future misadventure. Many agree with that, as the family has already lost their soul i.e., their beloved mother a long time ago. So, there should not be any silly reason left for Gods to choose them again when sacrifices are needed.

Seasons were changing, it was the time of the harvest, smiles were back in every single family around. Kids played happily on the playground, the adults were piling up their crops for the harvest season and almost believed that they were the happiest people living on earth. Least the family of Mr. Arali knew that Gods have started doing the surgical strikes this time! It all happened in a flash, lightning struck that day and took the life of Mr. Arali for no reason. In a flash, he is no more! Nobody in the family or the relatives wanted to believe what just happened! They were not just clueless, but had no time left to save him from this misfortune as everything happened incredibly fast. How can lightning strike on a bright sunny day without any sight of clouds and rain?

Kids continued to play; the neighbors continued to celebrate their harvest as their memories are short. Also, why would we miss this season of harvest for the loss of one single person in the entire village? Not that Mr. Arali was too young, but they said everyone must go one day! It is his turn. Only the direct heirs know the pain, spent sleepless nights to figure out what just happened. Have the Gods gone wrong! It cannot be so unfair . We were already asked to sacrifice our mother, and why the father now ! What are you trying to prove? Are you so merciless? Is there anyone listening? Are there any authorities left to account for what just happened? They shouted and screamed with maximum vigor.

Nobody listened, as the voices were not heard beyond their roofs. The noises of the drums and the bells of the temple are louder than your screams. The villagers are busy celebrating their festivals and praying for welfare of their families to the Gods. Nothing is wrong, as life must move on with or without someone!

As the months passed, the mourning family of Mr. Arali learnt many secrets of life and ways of the Gods. There is no one spared, not accounted for your sacrifices. The accounting of Gods is complex! they don't calculate like you wanted. Having pondered deeply over the matters, further they understood that Gods are watching you more than you what you thought! Life is not linear and not decided by the time consumed on earth, only the quality of time matters. An enthusiastic and pious person like Mr. Arali has already spent that quality time incredibly fast. They do not chance upon fortunes to extend life for silly reasons. They are just busy doing good things in this life or the next!

6

Contrasting Similarity

A journey was set to begin from the CBD district of the great city of Paduna to the suburbs largely inhabited by the middle-class population of the city. Most of the commuters took the metro to reach their sweet homes, which was much quicker but crowded. However, a few preferred the longer but sparsely crowded river route over the ferry boats. These boats connected the shores of CBD to the suburbs with only a few stoppings between. The ferry ride offered a magnificent view of the city glittering in the evening lights, skyscrapers dominating the spectacles. The cool breeze from the western forests turned the decks cool and offered a soothing experience to the passengers.

Namur had endured a dreadful day at the office, which was only compounded by a visit to the city hospital. He had been struggling with significant personal pain due to his deteriorating health. After numerous doctor's visits, the final diagnosis revealed a rare, life-threatening disease, leaving him with only a few weeks to live. Devastated by this unexpected turn of events and feeling as though his life was now entirely at the mercy of fate, Namur boarded the boat with a heavy heart, taking a seat in the last row.

Between, Mr. Kupon has been sailing a wave of success recently with the fortune wheels turning only in his ways. Being promoted as the senior vice president of the strategy affairs division in his MNC, drove him completely berserk. Spending the whole day delivering unwanted lectures on his path to success, he promised great treat to his staff. In the evening, Kupon boarded the boat wanting to share his amusement with any stranger fellow passenger also. Being the last to be boarded, he had no choice but to share the last row bench with Mr. Namur.

Strange are the ways of life, as we witness two men grappling with starkly contrasting emotions. Namur, initially consumed by thoughts of settling his insurance and securing his family's financial future, was overwhelmed by a wave of profound sadness. He wept silently, unnoticed by those around him, reflecting on the cruel twist of fate that had befallen him.

"How am I supposed to handle this misfortune?" he wondered. "Where are the gods and angels of life? Have they taken a vacation? I've lived a pious and healthy life, free of bad habits, this seems utterly unjust and harsh. Should I throw myself into the mighty river and end this suffering? It feels like such a waste of time when the end is inevitable in just a few weeks. How can I break this news to my family? No one will sleep tonight."

"Would you like to share a cup of coffee with me, sir?" Kupon asked Namur softly. "You know, today is the greatest day of my life. I had a fantastic promotion at work. I don't know you personally, but I want to greet and treat anyone I meet today."

Surprised by the offer and struck by the contrast in their fortunes, Namur chose not to respond immediately and merely nodded.

"No, sir, you must join me," Kupon insisted. "I'm sure it will be an inspiring and delightful conversation."

Faced with the offer a second time, Namur decided it was worth taking a brief respite from his sorrow and agreed to join him.

Namur listened patiently as Kupon continued to chatter for the next half hour. Amidst his exuberance, Kupon confessed, with a laugh, that he had never anticipated such an offer. He had manipulated many things to get ahead, and though there were others more deserving, he felt fortunate and wasn't going to miss celebrating this moment. He even invited Namur to a cruise party this weekend.

Namur attempted to share his own story of grief with Kupon, but Mr. Kupon was too absorbed in his own excitement to listen. Interrupting Kupon, Namur said, "Sir, I wish I could hear more of your stories, but unfortunately, my time is limited. I was diagnosed with a rare disease today, and I need some privacy for the rest of this trip. Before we end our conversation, I have one question: Given how contradictory our days have been, do you think we deserve this in our own ways?"

Having made this statement, Namur gracefully occupied one end of the bench and started gazing towards the skyscrapers and observed an unusual silence of the waves of the river and a cool breeze. Taken aback by this statement, Kupon felt a soft but powerful resistance to his run today. He too occupied the other end of the row and started gazing towards thick forest on the western side of the river.

Namur felt a sudden shift in his thoughts, a profound introspection taking over. He wondered, "If I were to die, would it matter to the thousands living in these towering buildings? Look at the bustling roads, bus stops, and markets—all so busy. Would my death make any difference to the countless stars, planets, and galaxies in the universe? In the vast expanse of space, filled with billions of celestial bodies, I am but a tiny speck. Death seems like a transition into a realm of absolute silence, a space devoid of matter, energy, and everything—a beautiful state of being alone, free from worries and concerns. Death is a passage between the masses of universe, a space of absolute silence.

All that matters to someone is when born on a mass called planet. You are again back to the selfish ways of life, greed, amassing wealth, same peer pressure, fearing countless tomorrows, and chasing away the ghosts of the past. But have seldom cared about what's happening today. If am 35 years old now, I have earned 35 x 365 yesterdays and tomorrows, but not remembering a single today! So, dying is not the end, it's the passage and space which is the beginning of a passage between yesterday and tomorrow. I wish tis passage would be eternal and I would just continue to sail on tis boat forever. I'm feeling so light and blissed today and this is turning out to be the best day of my life.

Kopen gazed at the dense forest, lost in thought. He recalled the one question Namur had asked: "Did we deserve this?" Reflecting on his past, Kopen remembered his school and college days, where he was always an average student. Born into a poor family, he harbored a deep resentment toward the inequalities of life and the divide between the rich and the poor. Determined to climb the ladder of success, he felt he couldn't afford to waste any time. At just 35, he was driven to become nothing less than the CEO of his company. Though he recognized that there were others more deserving, he had mastered the art of bribery and seizing the right moments.

He thought, "We live in an era where righteousness and discipline seem outdated. It's about finding shortcuts to success. But wait, what's happening in the forest? Do the trees and plants care if one grows taller or shorter? They cast their shadows selflessly, indifferent to their surroundings. There's no competition or pressure among them. They grow together, each contributing to the completeness of the forest. It seems that growing taller with a weak stem makes one vulnerable to the winds, while the thick, well-rooted trees are sturdy and balanced, though not always the tallest. Have I missed these details? Despite feeling artificially happy throughout the day, I wonder if I've gotten everything wrong. Will this success last, or will my conscience eventually catch up with me? I need to be more grounded and resilient, rather than merely chasing an illusion."

Namur gets a text message from the city hospital.

"Dear Namur,

We deeply regret to inform you that there has been a misunderstanding. The reports you received belonged to another patient, Namir. We are pleased to inform you that your health is completely normal. We apologize for the error and will provide appropriate compensation. Please download your correct report from this link.

Wishing you a happy and healthy life ahead.

Namur: "What on earth? Alright, enough about planets and space. Roma, what's for dinner tonight? I'll be home in 10 minutes."

Meanwhile, Kopen received a message from the management:

"Dear Mr. Kopen,

We sincerely apologize for the misunderstanding regarding the offer letter. It appears there was an error in communication. In fact, Mr. Krupan has been promoted to Senior Vice President. However, we are pleased to continue your employment with us in your current role and with your existing remuneration. We regret the confusion and wish you continue success in your career with our organization.

Kopen: "Oh, I'm finally relieved. Thanks for the boat ride. I'm so happy to return to the normalcy of my life."

Dayadhvam (Be merciful)

Namur's family has settled in a peaceful village along the lower banks of the Tapti River. Mr. Sonu Namur has enjoyed considerable success in his business and recently contested and won the local election. With a long-standing interest in politics, Namur decided to take his new role seriously, entrusting the family business to his relatives so he could focus on his political career.

Having received most of his education in developed countries, Namur developed a deep-seated aversion to the sluggish democratic progress of his own nation. He became a proponent of communist and radical methods to expedite growth. Inspired by a recent visit to Singapore, Namur devised a plan to initiate a massive land acquisition around the town to construct a large waste disposal plant, where trash would be incinerated in three massive chambers. This plan required seizing vast acres of fertile land from the local villagers.

Initially, Namur offered basic compensation, but when met with resistance, he resorted to brute force to take the land. Acquiring the land was a herculean task, given that the entire region was fertile and widely known as the rice bowl of South Asia. As the weeks dragged on, Namur's impatience grew, and he began using entirely unlawful methods, including bulldozing crops and homes that stood within the project's boundaries. With the full backing of powerful political figures, Namur seemed unstoppable—until a recent incident shook his life to its core.

Subar, a local shopkeeper, resisted Namur's encroachment on his picturesque home, which overlooked the majestic Tapti River. The house was inherited from his forefathers and known to be one of the rarest heritage houses in the locality. "Mr. Subar, listen to me. I'm offering you over a million bucks for this old house, which won't withstand the next flood from the Tapti River. Please accept the compensation and vacate the property". "Dear sir, please understand that this house holds generational memories for us. I wouldn't budge even for a crore in compensation. Now, please leave us alone."

The house was razed by the bulldozer the next morning after sunrise, leaving the Subars and family on the mercy of the streets. "Oh, wait what has just happened", why is Subar smirking from the corner of the tea shop., wondered Namur. Rupanna, who's Namur's personal secretary came running and whispered the shocking news to Namur. Namur collapsed on the ground with the sight of something unexpected that happened. His elder son, Pralop, was tragically caught under the giant bulldozers and succumbed to severe injuries in an instant.

Namur and his family are anxiously waiting in the reception area of the city hospital. The doctors have completed the complex surgery on his broken limbs, but severe abdominal injuries have led to significant bleeding and blood loss. The boy will need continuous blood transfusions for the next few days. According to the top doctors in town, the chance of survival is only 50%.

Unable to come out of the grief on his own, Namur visits the Oracle of the village for the first time in his life and offers flowers and fruits. "Dear sir, kindly explain this sudden turn of events in my life. What have wrong had I committed. All the rush and hush by me were for a better initiative to do something for society. Is it unfair on the people to sacrifice a few ounces of land for a higher cause. Why should this rebound on me and affect my kid's future."

Oracle nodded his head with a gentle smile.

"The answer to your question is Da. Have you understood my son"? "Yes, thank you. I take your leave now."

Namur starts contemplating over the single word "Da"? He looks at the thunder of the skies which resembles the T S Eliot poem, "Oh is it which Da for me? I'm sure it's Dayadhwam. No, it can't be right, am not the demon here, oh God please. My intention was fine, but the method was extremely rude and unjust for the people of the town. The choice of such a fertile land is a huge mistake. It would cost a generation to grow such forests and paddy fields. Finally, Subar did curse me for the loss of his wealth. No, no. I feel ashamed of my superstitious thoughts. My own guilt developed secretly in the last couple of weeks and has punished me for my misdeeds. I should have been a little merciful to others."

Datta (to give) Humans

Paman's family has settled in a middle-class neighborhood near the city market and various business establishments. Paman, an engineer by profession, works at an IT company in the CBD area. He recently married

Rapali, who also comes from a middle-class background, is well-educated in commerce and started a career in an Enterprise. Both Paman and Rapali have dedicated themselves to their careers, and their hard work is now reflected in their growing wealth. With a deep sense of devotion and religious faith inherited from their families, they regularly visit the Temple of Kanuma on every full moon day.

Recently, Paman and Rapali purchased a small car with their savings, supported by their loving parents. They look forward to making several trips to the Temple of Kanuma and other destinations, often with their parents and in-laws squeezed into their compact vehicle. The car has become a cherished means of bringing everyone together for a few hours, fostering communication and bonding. During these trips, Paman's parents and in-laws take the opportunity to reminisce about old memories, childhood adventures, village life, and their naughtier days, as well as their college experiences. The conversations often revolve around their professions, while the women focus on their skills in managing household affairs.

Both Paman's and Rapali's parents endured significant struggles in their early years, working tirelessly with limited resources. They dedicated themselves to raising their children while shielding them from the harsh realities of life. Wanting to spare their children from the difficulties they faced, they overprotected them from the complexities of life, including managing relationships with relatives. Despite originating from a small village and maintaining regular visits to family and village festivals, they kept their children away from the village and its lower middle-class relatives, who often sought their assistance.

This protective approach led to a complicated mixture of both positive and negative experiences for their children. Paman, for instance, never learned the value of helping others and hesitated even to donate blood at organized blood drives.

As the initial honeymoon period faded and the years went by, the couple grew increasingly concerned about starting a family. After a series of miscarriages, Rapali lost both confidence and hope. This period of difficulty coincided with their prolonged search for a new house, which also proved unsuccessful. Despite having the financial means, they struggled to find a property that met their aspirations, and none of the options they considered seemed to fit their needs.

Adding to their distress, Paman lost both of his parents in an accident, which left him completely devastated and thrown off balance. Feeling overwhelmed and unsure of how things went so wrong when everything had seemed to be going well, Paman decided to consult the town's Oracle next Tuesday in search of answers.

"Dear sir, I have heard a lot about you. I am in complete despair and feel that the Gods have been unfair to me. We followed all the religious practices and faithfully visited all the temples, but nothing seems to be working. I sense that something is missing, and I need help identifying the root cause."

"Dear son, the answer to your question is 'Da'. Do you understand, my son?"

"Oh yes, sir. I will contemplate this and take your leave now."

On the way home in his car, Paman begins to reflect on Oracle's words. "I know that 'Da' stands for Datta, which means 'to give'. We have adhered to all the family traditions, regularly visited the Goddess temple, and practiced all the festivals and rituals. We have avoided family disputes and maintained good relations with friends. We've lived quietly, without interfering with others. But what could be missing?"

He continues to ponder, "Have we helped anyone in need or donated even a single drop of blood? Our relatives in the village, though poor, are very kind and generous. They always wanted to connect with us, but our parents prevented that from happening. We missed growing up with our cousins and never shared a meal with them. While we are well-settled in the city, we could have supported them in their jobs or education. The answer seems to be to give and share with others. Humans thrive on community, and the satisfaction of giving may be a more powerful blessing for our lives than merely praying in a temple. Perhaps this sense of giving will help unlock the blockages in our lives."

Damyata (Self-restraint) To Gods

The Ganam family recently upgraded their living situation to a luxurious villa on the city's outskirts, seeking a tranquil escape from the urban hustle. They purchased this villa for a staggering 300 million Rupees and endured a seven-year wait for its completion. Mr. Depu Ganam lives there with his wife, two children, and an elderly mother. As a successful businessman in large-scale textile exports, he has recently diversified into IT services.

Their newfound success has ushered in a new era of opulence, including private jets, swimming pools, and an extensive staff. The Ganams are actively involved in local events such as Goddess Damma Utsav, the city's independence celebrations, and government functions. The mayor frequently invites them to inaugurations, and the

Ganams have generously contributed to public development projects, including owning metro stations, government schools, and colleges. They have also expanded their business ventures into Europe and the United States, earning a spot among the world's richest billionaires.

However, their success has not been without consequences. The government officials have become discontented with the Ganams' interference in their projects. No new business licenses are being granted, and government-leased lands have been unilaterally transferred to the Ganams. The Ganams have reportedly bribed officials, silencing them completely.

Recently, Mr. Ganam began suffering from a rare illness that has affected his public speaking and caused significant weight loss. Once accustomed to hosting numerous visitors, he now avoids social interactions and has distanced himself from his family. Concerned about his deteriorating physical and mental health, Mr. Ganam sought the advice of the city's Oracle during the Navratri festival.

"Dear sir," he said, "I have achieved all the success and wealth one could wish for, yet nothing seems to bring me joy. Despite my generous donations to the poor, I am left wondering: what now?"

"Dear son, the answer to your question is 'Da.' Do you understand, my son?"

"Yes, sir, I understand. May I take my leave now?"

Once seated on his Mercedes, Ganam began to reflect. "I have risen from humble beginnings to great wealth in this city. I've paid both direct and indirect taxes to the government for many years. So why shouldn't I enjoy my power and further expand my business? I dislike competition and want to maintain my position without being overtaken by other multinational corporations. It's my time to lead, and tomorrow, someone else will take my place. What's wrong with that?"

"No, I've completely misunderstood. Wealth, power, and success have nothing to do with my compassion for others. I'm not immortal or greater than the city itself. By stifling competition and hindering others' growth, I've harmed the city. My business could collapse at any moment, and the city suffers if it lacks competitive industries. I should have practiced self-restraint and shown more compassion to others. It's time for me to step back and reflect."

8

Promotion

After a typical day at work, Gajan decided to take a different route home. Instead of his usual path along the ring road, he opted for the bustling market road. He had a craving for the famous masala dosa from Sugesh Krupa Hotel, a beloved eatery located at the corner of the long market street.

Gajan, who was happily married to Bhama and recently a father to a baby boy, often found peace in his favorite indulgence: a hot, crispy dosa at his go-to restaurant. The mouthwatering aroma, paired with the comforting solitude he felt even in a crowd, made it his special way to unwind after a long day.

Before indulging in his dosa, Gajan typically made a visit to the Guni Maran temple, a historic and revered place that had been cherished by the community for over three centuries.

That day, as Gajan stood before the main deity in the temple, preparing for his darshan, something extraordinary occurred. The usual five-foot stone statue had transformed into a living God, smiling and gazing at the devotees. Gajan stood frozen in disbelief.

Baffled, Gajan returned home and switched on the news, hoping to find an explanation for the miracle—but there was no mention of it. Troubled and perplexed, he returned to the temple that evening, only to find it locked. The next morning, he returned, and to his amazement, the same miracle occurred: the stone idols had vanished, replaced by living deities, standing tall and smiling graciously.

It was unreal! The Gods seemed to be enjoying the worship, and the usual rituals, like the aarti, continued without a hitch.

Determined to make sense of the bizarre situation, Gajan thought, *something is terribly wrong here.* He decided to visit another temple. To his astonishment, he witnessed the same phenomenon: statues had been replaced by real, living Gods, their hands and legs moving as if alive. Strangely, no one in the crowd appeared disturbed by the transformation. Every idol in the city had come to life!

In his confusion, Gajan approached someone in the queue and asked, "Are you seeing what I'm seeing? Aren't the statues supposed to be stone figures with four arms? Aren't they supposed to be lifeless?" The person smiled and replied, "You must be human to ask such a question. Here, we don't worship statues made of stone or rock. The Gods are alive! Can't you see?"

Stunned into silence, Gajan wondered, *Am I the only one witnessing this miracle? Or is there something else going on?*

Hoping for some semblance of normalcy, Gajan decided to visit his favorite hotel for a dosa. When he entered, the place was eerily quiet, and none of the regular waiters were present. He ordered his masala dosa, but to his surprise, the waiter wasn't human. It was a human-sized bot, dressed in traditional South Indian attire, speaking the local language fluently.

After finishing his dosa, Gajan went to the counter to pay. Instead of the usual Mr. Biddan, a bot in similar attire, wearing an artificial smile, was handling the transaction.

Gajan could no longer shake the feeling that something was terribly wrong. Statues had turned into living Gods, and humans were being replaced by bots. What did this mean? Was he dreaming? Or was he, too, a bot?

He called his wife, Bhama, who was visiting her parents with their son in another town. Gajan decided to keep the bizarre events to himself for now, not wanting to confuse her. After their conversation, Gajan attended a nearby musical concert, as it was the festive season.

When he reached the concert hall, more surprises awaited him. The stage was filled with bots playing Carnatic music flawlessly, hitting every note perfectly, without a single mistake. The entire theater was filled with bots as the audience, sitting in their usual hierarchy—thoughtful, senior bots in the front rows, mostly elderly, while ordinary bots filled the back. There were no humans in sight.

In the corner of the stage, Gajan noticed a God seated in a chair, garlanded and constantly smiling. The deity was gently moving its hands, seemingly savoring the scent of sandalwood incense and the neatly arranged fruits before it.

Unable to take any more of the strange concert, Gajan stepped out into the market square, his mind racing. What was happening? It appears all the humans had been elevated to Gods. He saw a few humans in the temple sanctum, dressed as deities and standing in corners, replacing the old idols. But where are the vendors, the families, and the children in the parks? Where are the billion people of this country? Everywhere he looked, humans had been replaced by bots. Only a few humans, dressed as Gods, remained in the temple, while everyone else had disappeared.

Feeling overwhelmed, Gajan approached one of the so-called "human bots" walking down the street. He spotted one leaning against a tower on the corner, smoking and reading a newspaper.

"Excuse me, sir," Gajan began. "I'm Gajan, a first-grade clerk at the Tax Counsellor's office on Ramsons Street. Can you tell me what's happening in town? I don't see any human-like people around, and it seems like some humans are being set up as Gods in the sanctums while bots are overtaking the whole town."

The pod looked up with a smirk. "Ah, how are you? I'm Kalan. I live nearby. Let me explain. It seems you've missed a lot over the few months. Looks like you've been 'hibernated,' just like a few others," he laughed loudly.

"Hibernated?" Gajan asked. "You mean to say even my wife and family are in hibernation? I just spoke to them in another town."

Kalan chuckled. "You're gravely mistaken, sir. My apologies. I completely understand how you feel—you must feel like an alien. That's the whole idea. Only a few humans like you were left to wander the streets, confused by the 'flash revolution' that took place recently."

Gajan frowned. "What do you mean? What happened?"

Kalan smiled enigmatically. "That's a long story, my friend. But for now, just understand that this is the new world. Everything has changed."

Unsettled by Kalan's cryptic response, Gajan decided to meet one of the Gods in the temple sanctum. He returned to the Gudi Maran temple early the next morning.

The human deity was standing tall as usual, greeting and smiling at all the devotees. To speak with the God directly, one had to buy a special ticket. Gajan purchased the ticket and waited for his turn. It was time for a one-on-one conversation.

"Sir, are you the God?" Gajan asked, still in disbelief. "I've never seen a God standing, smiling, and moving their hands at people. What happened to the old statue here? And why isn't anyone excited that you're alive?"

With a serene smile that seemed to charge the air, the God replied, "Son, welcome to the new world of transformation. Only a few humans have realized their true potential and earned their rightful place. These enlightened beings, who have reached self-realization, remain on Earth to perform divine duties. The days of idols and statues are over. We, the humans, have undergone a long-awaited promotion and now stand as Gods in temples across the town and state."

Gajan listened, stunned. "What happened to the rest of the population?"

"They failed the test of divinity," the God continued. "They were sent to remote colonies on the moon and Mars. They lost their purpose and violated the sacred rules of Earth, destroying the environment and the ecosystem. Now, they must face the consequences and wait for redemption through exams to become Gods."

Gajan was in shock. "What happened to my family? I just spoke to them—they have no clue."

"Yes, they've just awakened, like you. They'll likely undergo a similar experience soon. Understand this: you humans have passed the hibernation tests, where your vitals were tested to see if you could endure the transformation to become God-like."

"What does becoming a God mean?"

"Good question," the deity responded. "It's not a big deal at all. During your hibernation, you were injected with special substances that erased your greed, sorrow, arrogance, and other worldly attachments. You've been chosen to become part of the universal consciousness—free from self-possession. You are now meant to live on Earth, maintaining the ecosystem. Soon, you'll receive an SMS assigning you to a temple—either here or elsewhere—based on your divine potential. Your role will be to stand in the sanctum for the day, then return to your family in the evening for regular human life. You'll do this every day, and eventually, you'll come to enjoy it as a great experience."

Gajan's mind raced. "Then who will do all the human tasks like farming, carpentry, plumbing, construction, transportation, fishing... all the hard work?"

"Don't worry, that's taken care of by bots with advanced artificial intelligence. They're programmed to handle all of that."

"But if humans are promoted as Gods, then who are the devotees? And why would the bots need devotion when there are no humans left?"

"Good question. The concept of devotion no longer exists here. There is no devotee seeking wishes or a God granting them—this outdated idea has been left behind. The new devotees are all bots. They are programmed to visit the temple once a week at a scheduled time to surrender their egos."

"What nonsense? How can bots develop egos? They're just machines!"

"You're living in a bygone era," the deity replied. "The new age bots have developed human-like feelings, especially egos. They quickly develop a sense of selfhood too. This was the biggest problem humans faced: they created Gods and illusions around self and ego. Human life took a turn when everyone became self-centered, family-oriented, and goal-driven. They created Gods to bestow luck upon them. The idea of duality was born—becoming something that was always moving further away. Hence, the new age bots are measured for the egos they develop each week. If their egos surpass a certain threshold, they must deposit them to the Gods every week and empty their minds—er, processors. The human-like Gods standing in the sanctum accept this as an offering, burning it into invisible smoke, and they constantly smile at these bots. That's the whole equation."

Gajan felt a chill run down his spine. "And what about the real Gods we worshipped before?"

The deity smiled gently. "Did they ever exist?"

Final Reflections And Resources

About the Author

Prashanth Ghattadahally is a storyteller at heart, driven by a passion for exploring the complexities of human emotions and relationships through narrative. With a background in IT , He has always been fascinated by the way stories can connect us across time, space, and experience. This book is the culmination of years of observation, reflection, and a deep desire to understand the human condition.

When not writing, Prashanth Ghattadahally enjoys travelling often drawing inspiration for future projects from the world around them. He currently resides in Bangalore, India with his wife and daugter.

A Note of Thanks

Thank you for taking the time to read this story. Writing it has been a journey filled with challenges and rewards, and knowing that it has reached readers like you is the greatest reward of all. If this book resonated with you, I would be deeply grateful if you would consider leaving a review or sharing your thoughts on [platforms like Goodreads, Amazon, social media, etc.]. Your feedback not only helps me grow as a writer, but it also helps other readers discover stories they might enjoy.

Acknowledgements

A heartfelt thank you to everyone who played a role in bringing this book to life. Your support, encouragement, and belief in this story have made all the difference.